The HEART of COMMUNICATION
Workbook

Workbook provides readers with practical tools and strategies they can use to improve their communication skills and build stronger, more positive relationships with others through inner healing.

Dr. Sandra W. Ingram

XULON PRESS

Xulon Press
555 Winderley Pl, Suite 225
Maitland, FL 32751
407.339.4217
www.xulonpress.com

© 2023 by Dr. Sandra W. Ingram

All rights reserved solely by the author. The author guarantees all contents are original and do not infringe upon the legal rights of any other person or work. No part of this book may be reproduced in any form without the permission of the author.

Due to the changing nature of the Internet, if there are any web addresses, links, or URLs included in this manuscript, these may have been altered and may no longer be accessible. The views and opinions shared in this book belong solely to the author and do not necessarily reflect those of the publisher. The publisher therefore disclaims responsibility for the views or opinions expressed within the work.

Paperback ISBN-13: 978-1-66288-394-1
Ebook ISBN-13: 978-1-66288-395-8

WELCOME

Welcome to this interactive workbook on communication in relationships! This workbook is designed to help you strengthen your relationships with others by improving your communication skills and developing inner healing. In this workbook, you will find exercises and activities to help you learn how to communicate effectively, resolve conflicts, and build strong connections with those around you. By the end of this workbook, you will have the tools you need to communicate more effectively and build healthier relationships.

INTRODUCTION

This relationship coaching workbook is designed to help individuals and couples build strong and healthy relationships. The workbook includes a series of questions and exercises that will guide you through the procedure of improving your communication, strengthening your connection, and creating a more fulfilling relationship.

Effective communication is a skill that is learned and improved with practice. This workbook provides the tools and techniques to enhance your communication skills and develop positive relationships with others. By applying these concepts in your personal and professional life, you will become an effective communicator in all aspects of your life.

By working through the questions and exercises in this self-reflection workbook, you will gain a deeper understanding of your communication style, fears in the relationship, how to embrace change, and your definition of communication. Use this knowledge to improve your communication skills and build stronger and healthier relationships with your partner. Remember, effective communication is the foundation of a successful relationship.

How to Use this Workbook:

To get the best results from this workbook, begin by reading the instructions in each section and understand the purpose of the exercises and how to complete them effectively. Reflect on the questions and prompts presented in each section and provide honest and thoughtful responses that reflect your practices and needs. There are no right or wrong answers, just your honest feedback. Feel free to use the space provided on each page to jot down answers to the questions and add additional thoughts and ideas.

Take advantage of the calendar provided, and jot down the accomplishments you completed and those you did not. You should carry over the ones you did not accomplish.

Use the workbook consistently to track your progress and revisit your responses periodically to gauge improvements and reassess your goals as needed. Next, create an action plan by breaking down your goals into actionable steps, setting timelines, considering potential obstacles, and creating strategies to overcome them. Next, put your action plan into practice by committing to regularly evaluating your progress and adjusting as needed. Be kind to yourself throughout the process and celebrate your accomplishments, no matter how small. Enjoy the process.

Daily practice: Affirmations and meditations are in the appendix. Be sure to write your accomplishments on the monthly calendar. Find something positive to be thankful for every day.

TABLE OF CONTENTS

Section #1: Understanding Communication 8
   1.1 What is Communication? 8
   1.2 Communication Barriers 9
   1.3 Importance of Effective Communication 9
   1.4 Reflection Question 10

Section #2: Five Types of Effective Communication (2-3 pages) .12
   2.1 Keys to Active Listening 12
   2.2 Types of Communication 13
   2.3 Reflection Question 15

Section #3: Communication Styles 17
   3.1 Styles of Communication 17
   3.2 Identifying your Communication Style 18
   3.3 Reflection Question 20

Section #4: Blame and Responsibility 21
   4.1 Definition 21
   4.2 Negative Effects 21
   4.3 Alternative Approaches 22
   4.4 "I" Statements 22
   4.5 Reflection Question 24

Section #5: Fear and Unforgiveness 26
   5.1 Definition 26
   5.2 Types of Fear 27
   5.3 Causes of Fear 27
   5.4 Effects of Fear 27
   5.5 Overcoming Fear 27
   5.6 Building Trust 28
   5.7 Reflection Question 29

Section #6: Self-Awareness ... 31
6.1 Definition ... 31
6.2 Benefits ... 31
6.3 Naikan Theory ... 31
6.4 Reference Question ... 33

Section #7: Mind Reset ... 35
7.1 Definition ... 35
7.2 Benefits of Mind Reset ... 35
7.3 Techniques for Mind Reset ... 35
7.4 Overcoming Mental Blocks/Limiting Beliefs ... 36
7.5 Reflection Question ... 37

Section #8: Conflict Resolution ... 39
8.1 Definition ... 39
8.2 Sources of Conflict ... 39
8.3 Strategies for Finding Common Ground ... 39
8.4 Conflict Resolution Skills ... 40
8.5 Reflection Question ... 41

Section #9: Embracing Change ... 43
9.1 The Nature of Change ... 43
9.2 Benefits of Change ... 43
9.3 Struggles of Change ... 44
9.4 Growth Mindset ... 44
9.5 Reflection Question ... 45

Section #10 – Inner Healing ... 46
10.1 Definition ... 46
10.2 Connection Between Past and Present ... 46
10.3 Reflection Question ... 48

BEFORE YOU BEGIN

Answer the following questions

RELATIONSHIP GOALS AND PLANNING

1. What are your three relationship goals?

   _____
   _____
   _____

2. What are some steps that you can take to achieve your relationship goals?

   _____
   _____
   _____

Self-Assessment- See Appendix 1

SECTION #1
Understanding Communication

"I know you think you understand what you thought I said, but I'm not sure you realize that what you heard is not what I meant." — Alan Greenspan

Section 1.1: This section of the workbook introduces the topic of effective communication, which refers to the process of exchanging information, thoughts, feelings, and ideas in a manner that is clear, respectful, and effective. It involves both verbal and non-verbal communication, including spoken words, tone of voice, body language, facial expressions, and gestures.

PURPOSE OF COMMUNICATION		
1. Expressing needs and desires.	3. Resolving conflicts.	5. Providing support and validation.
2. Sharing emotions and feelings.	4. Building trust and connection.	6. Sharing values and goals

Expressing needs and desires, both positive and negative, allows couples to express their wants, expectations, and perspectives while working towards mutual satisfaction, emotional intimacy, and understanding.

Sharing emotions and feelings: Effective communication enables partners to share their emotions openly, positive, and negative, which fosters emotional intimacy and understanding.

Resolving conflicts plays a crucial role in allowing couples to express their concerns, listen to each other's viewpoints, and find mutually acceptable resolutions.

Building trust and connections is the gateway to honest communication, strengthening faith, and deepening the emotional connection between couples. It creates a safe space for vulnerability and fosters a sense of being understood and supported.

Providing support and validation: Communication offers emotional support, validation, and empathy by allowing couples to actively listen, provide comfort, and be present for each other during challenging times.

Sharing values and goals: Partners should communicate their values, dreams, and aspirations, which allows them to align their visions and work towards common goals as a team.

1.2 Communication Barriers

One of the biggest difficulties in relationships is thinking communication has taken place when it has not. This is an illusion.

Appendix 3 Communication Barriers
Effective communication in relationships involves active listening, empathy, clarity, and respectful expression of thoughts and emotions. It requires being present, attentive, and responsive to your partner's communication while striving to understand their perspective and still expressing your own in a constructive and considerate manner.

1.3 Remember these three things to make yourself a better communicator:

- Be responsible for your thoughts, actions, words, and feelings.

- Keep your eyes on the prize- better communication- and focus on how to make improvements in communication.

- Take ownership of your feelings and openly communicate with honesty by acknowledging that you are flawed and do not have all the answers. When you acknowledge your prejudices, how you hurt your spouse, and take ownership of your decisions whether good or bad, you advance your communication by one hundred percent.

THREE GOALS OF BETTER COMMUNICATION (Example: spending more quality time together):

Action Steps: How will you implement the goals you set?

_____
_____
_____

1.4 Reflection Question:
Why is achieving my goals important?

_____
_____
_____

When I achieve this goal, what will success look like?

_____
_____
_____

How will I benefit from reaching this goal?

1. _____
2. _____
3. _____

See Appendix 2 Accomplishment Sheet

Fill out daily, and record on the calendar.

MONDAY	TUESDAY	WEDNESDAY	THURSDAY	FRIDAY	SATURDAY	SUNDAY
1	2	3	4	5	6	7
8	9	10	11	12	13	14
15	16	17	18	19	20	21
22	23	24	25	26	27	28
29	30	31				

Write five goals on the calendar that you want to achieve this month, and at the end of the month, check off the goals you achieved and move the ones you did not achieve to the next month.

SECTION #2
Five Types of Effective Communication

"I have learned the more I know and understand myself, the more I know and understand my spouse." — Dr. Sandra Ingram

To become a better communicator, you must understand five facets of communication (verbal, nonverbal, written, listening, and visual) and how they contribute to what you say, how you say it, and why you say it.

The more we know ourselves and how we communicate, the better we can know that our spouse has different communication types. With this awareness, we can at least have some idea of why they are communicating the way they do.

Communication is a fundamental pillar of a healthy relationship and involves both speaking and actively listening. It requires you to be open, honest, and vulnerable while clearly expressing your thoughts and needs respectfully.

2.1 Keys to active listening

Practice these skills that improve communication by giving your full attention, summarizing what is being said, and asking clarifying questions.

Being an active listener is imperative because hearing is not listening. Active listening involves being fully invested in the conversation, mind, body, and soul. In other words, you are all in and focused with no distractions. You should learn to follow the following keys to active listening.

- **Avoid interrupting** or becoming defensive during conversations.

- **Be mindful of your tone and non-verbal cues,** as they can influence how your message is received.

- **Use "I" statements** to express your own feelings and avoid blaming or accusing language. (Discussed in section 4)

- **Acknowledge and discuss positive and negative emotions,** as suppressing them can lead to resentment.

- **Address conflicts calmly and constructively** focusing on finding solutions rather than winning arguments.

- **Compromise** and finding common ground are essential for resolving differences.

- **Regularly check in** with your partner to ensure you feel heard, understood, and supported.

- **Be patient and understanding** when your partner shares their thoughts and feelings, even if you disagree.

- **Seek professional help** or counseling if communication issues persist or become difficult to manage.

2.2 Types of Communication

- **In verbal communication**, language is used in sentences or phrases to relay thoughts or feelings. The downside is that words are often misunderstood, so to keep comments from being misunderstood, it is best, when you speak, to watch for hints the other person is accepting or in agreement with what you are saying. A hint may include a head nod or a smile. That is where *nonverbal communication* comes in.

- **Nonverbal communication** involves what is not displayed instead of what is displayed. Nonverbal communication includes facial expressions, posture, frowning, or walking away.

- **Listening** is the most valuable communication tool in the arsenal of resources. Hearing and listening are very different. You can hear without really listening. When you communicate, be fully engaged, mind and body. Listening attentively shows your spouse that you respect what they are saying, and in return, they will learn to respect what you are saying.

- **Written communication** is indicated when you do not wish to face your spouse because their nonverbal communication intimidates you (frowning), writing it down is an option. Just be short and to the point, and only address the issue at hand; this is not the time to write a novel or complain about everything you always wanted to get off your chest.

- **Visual communication** involves communication through the things expressed with a numerical value (paycheck). Men fall into this category because they are concerned with the tangible and not the emotional. For them, communicating their love takes a material or physical form. Because men concentrate on the physical, they like to give flowers and gifts, bring home a paycheck, fix stuff around the house, and take you to dinner. Men not only like to express themselves visually, but they like to receive visually. Physical or visual communication shows up as men wanting their partners to cook their favorite foods, look sexy, bring home their dry cleaning, and have the house looking nice. Understanding these behaviors, both giving and receiving are valuable for women to acknowledge. You don't have to agree with it but be aware of this communication style.

What are the three goals of your becoming an active listener? Why is it important?

_____

_____

_____

Which type of communication best describes you and why?

_____

_____

_____

Action Steps: List three steps you will implement to change or improve your listening.

1. _____

2. _____

3. _____

2.3 Reflection Question

What are the greatest challenges of good communication (for example: not being respected)?

_____

_____

_____

Use the chart in Appendix 5 (Signs of poor communication) to identify your top three poor communication skills).

Appendix 2
Daily Accomplishment Sheet

Monthly Calendar

Write five goals on the calendar that you want to achieve this month, and at the end of the month, check off the goals you achieved and move the ones you did not achieve to the next month.

MONDAY	TUESDAY	WEDNESDAY	THURSDAY	FRIDAY	SATURDAY	SUNDAY
1	2	3	4	5	6	7
8	9	10	11	12	13	14
15	16	17	18	19	20	21
22	23	24	25	26	27	28
29	30	31				

SECTION #3
Communication Styles

"Communication works for those who work at it."–John Powel

The styles of communication are passive, aggressive, passive-aggressive, and assertive.

Now that you understand the types of communication, explore the different styles – passive, aggressive, passive-aggressive, and assertive. Identify your communication style, understanding that most people are a combination of types, not just one.

My communication style is _____.

3.1 Styles of Communication

- In **passive communication**, you ignore your rights and allow others to do the same, which may lead to anger and resentment because you are holding things in. Avoidance of conflict is a feature of this style of communication. Everyone and their opinion comes before yours. You commit communication suicide.

- In **aggressive communication**, you and what you feel, and think are most important, even at the expense of others and their feelings. People in this category are usually hostile and hurt others by their ways or actions. The aggressive person pushes others away; it is all about them. This style of communication is detrimental to a relationship. The characteristics of an aggressive communicator are blaming, dominating, and use of threats or intimidation.

- In the **passive-aggressive communication** style, you are calm on the surface but angry on the inside. This person displays, avoids communication, and has limited consideration for their spouse. They are ready to explode at any moment. The characteristics of passive-aggressive communication are expressing negative feelings indirectly, using sarcasm or backhanded compliments, and avoiding-confrontation.

- **Assertive** communication does not mean you come in like a bulldozer and plow everything down because you want to make your point. You stand up for yourself and your own needs and wants while keeping in mind the wants and needs of others. The characteristics of assertive communication are expressing one's needs and opinions clearly. The benefits of proactive communication are improved relationships, increased self-confidence, and reduced stress and anxiety.

3.2 Identifying Your Communication Style

Here is a tip for identifying your communication style:
Obtain self-reflection, feedback from others, etc. (not just your friends and family).
Be honest with yourself and dig deep into who you are.

COMMUNICATION STYLES			
Passive	Aggressive	Passive-Aggressive	Assertive

What three goals do you wish to obtain after determining your communication style?
_____
_____
_____

What steps will you take to adjust your style if needed?
_____
_____
_____

What do you believe is your communication style, and why?
_____
_____
_____

List three examples that illustrate your communication style.

1. _____

2. _____

3. _____

Monthly calendar

Write five goals on the calendar that you want to achieve this month and at the end of the month, check off the goals you achieved and move the ones you did not achieve to the next month.

MONDAY	TUESDAY	WEDNESDAY	THURSDAY	FRIDAY	SATURDAY	SUNDAY
1	2	3	4	5	6	7
8	9	10	11	12	13	14
15	16	17	18	19	20	21
22	23	24	25	26	27	28
29	30	31				

Appendix 2
Daily Accomplishment Sheet

3.3 Reflection Question: What would you want to change about your communication style?

_____

_____

_____

SECTION #4
Blame and Responsibility

"Stop the blame game. Stop! Stop looking out the window and look in the mirror!"
—Eric Thomas

In this section, you will explore the concept of blame and how it impacts your relationships. You will learn to take responsibility for your actions and avoid blaming others for problems in your relationships.

4.1 Definition

Blame is the art of making others responsible for all the problematic things that happen to us. In other words, blame is self-serving. You take the credit when things go right and blame others when things go wrong. So why are we compelled to do it? There are several reasons: it is less work for us, we do not have to be held accountable, it protects us from feeling helpless or vulnerable, but most of all, it fuels our reason to be right (we want to be in control). When you practice blame, it implies you do not have faith in yourself as a communicator and you must find fault in your spouse.

4.2 Negative Effects

The real issue with blame is that it only affects the person who is doing the blaming. It can create inaction on your part because you believe the solution is in the other person's hands. Therefore, blame holds back real change.

If you blame others, there is no inner reflection. Like Eric Thomas said, "Stop the blame game. "Stop! Stop looking out the window and look in the mirror." The mirror can only reflect what it sees, not what you want it to see. Most of us see ourselves in a different light than others. That is because we concentrate on our good points and not our faults.

Blame feeds your need to be in control or the illusion of being in control. Why is power-important to you? Power-is important to you because it fuels your reason to be correct and absolves you of being accountable for your actions. Not blaming someone means you must accept there was a situation where you did not act in a way you were proud of. Your mouth flew open before your brain engaged.

Understand the role blame plays in the relationship. It helps you to unload the emotional pain that you feel but suppress. Do not suppress your pain because, if it is not expressed at the appropriate time, it will show up in another place and time, and you will be wondering why you said that when it has nothing to do with the current conversation.

The real issue with blame is that it only affects the person who is doing the blaming. It can create inaction on your part because you believe the solution is in the other person's hands. Therefore, blame holds back real change.

4.3 Alternative Approaches

Now that we have some knowledge of blame, what it is, and how it affects you and your spouse, how do we stop the blame game? The first thing to do is own some part of the problem (I did not say all but some part). Flip blame by trying to understand others better.

By understanding yourself, you realize that blame for most of us is a habit. It is our default (comfort zone) reaction to conflict. Most of us do not like conflict and try to always avoid conflict.

4.4 "I" Statements

Use "I" statements to express your own feelings and avoid blaming or accusing language.

"I" Statements: This exercise involves using "I" statements instead of "you" statements when communicating with your partner. For example, instead of saying, "You never listen to me," say, "I feel unheard when we talk. "I" statements help to express feelings without blaming the other person.

THREE PARTS OF "I" STATEMENTS

I feel _____ (emotion)

when _____ (another person does or does not do what was expected)

because _____ (I think it means)

Give three examples of using "I" statements in your relationships.

_____

_____

_____

List three causes of your blame (control).

_____

_____

_____

List three goals to explore feelings of blame (Example: I will be more empathetic and understanding).

_____

_____

_____

Action Steps: How will you implement the goals?

_____

_____

_____

I blame others because.

_____
_____
_____

4.5 Reflection Question:
Why do you think you blame others? When you blame, how are you feeling (mad, angry, etc.)?

_____
_____
_____

See Appendix 2
Daily Accomplishment Sheet

Monthly Calendar

Write five goals on the calendar that you want to achieve this month and at the end of the month, check off the goals you achieved and move the ones you did not achieve to the next month.

MONDAY	TUESDAY	WEDNESDAY	THURSDAY	FRIDAY	SATURDAY	SUNDAY
1	2	3	4	5	6	7
8	9	10	11	12	13	14
15	16	17	18	19	20	21
22	23	24	25	26	27	28
29	30	31				

SECTION #5
Fear and Unforgiveness

"Forgiveness is not an occasional act; it is a constant attitude."
Martin Luther King, Jr.

In this section, you will learn the importance of forgiveness in relationships.-and explore the different types of forgiveness. Additionally, you will grasp the impact of fear in the relationship.

5.1 Definition

Remember, fear is false evidence appearing real. Become friends with and embrace your fear. Why? Because greatness includes fear. Take notice and remember, where you place your attention, you place your intention.

Fear can significantly impact relationships, causing distance, mistrust, and emotional disconnection. It can manifest as abandonment, rejection, intimacy, or vulnerability, leading to defensive behaviors and emotional walls that hinder the growth and depth of relationships.

To identify your fears, reflect on past experiences or patterns that may have contributed to your fears. By acknowledging and understanding fears, you can address them and work towards healing and growth.

Being open and honest is crucial in addressing fear in relationships. Express your fears, worries and concerns, allowing there to be a safe space to share vulnerabilities. This can foster understanding and empathy and help build trust and emotional intimacy.

Trust is essential in overcoming fear and deepening relationships. Consistency, reliability, and open communication contribute to building trust. Be dependable and demonstrate through your actions that you can be trusted.

Unforgiveness can create emotional barriers and resentment in essential to recognize the impact of holding onto grudges and the benefits of forgiveness. Forgiveness is not condoning hurtful actions but rather a personal choice to let go of negative emotions and seek healing and reconciliation.

It is crucial to understand and process your emotions. Allow yourself to experience and express your feelings, and then work towards letting go of resentment and bitterness. This may involve seeking therapy, engaging in forgiveness practices, or seeking support from trusted individuals.

Cultivate empathy and understanding towards your partner's perspective and experiences. Recognize that everyone makes mistakes, and holding onto unforgiveness can hinder personal growth and relationships. Practice empathy by putting yourself in their shoes and their motivations and struggles.

Love yourself and recognize that you are human and capable of making mistakes as well. Learn from your mistakes, take responsibility for your actions, and work towards self-growth and personal development.

Addressing fear and unforgiveness in relationships is a journey of healing and growth. It requires patience, self-reflection, and a commitment to personal development. Engage in self-reflection, journaling, or mindfulness to support your healing process.

Overcoming fear and unforgiveness can lead to the rebuilding and strengthening of relationships. Addressing these issues creates a space for trust, empathy, and deeper connection to flourish. Celebrate small victories along the way and appreciate the progress made in the relationship.

5.2 Types of Fear
Rejection, abandonment, intimacy, conflict.

5.3 Causes of fear
Past traumas or negative experiences, low self-esteem, or a lack of trust.

5.4 Effects of fear
Apprehension leads to defensive behavior, poor communication, and a lack of intimacy.

5.5 Overcoming fear
Active listening, healthily expressing emotions and using "I" statements instead of "you" statements.
Confront it and work through it.

💛 5.6 Building Trust

Be honest and open, follow through on commitments, and show empathy and understanding.

List three Reasons why you should forgive (Example: Self-healing)

_____
_____
_____

Goals of overcoming fear (it signifies growth)

_____
_____
_____

Action Steps How will you implement the goals you stated to forgive?

_____
_____
_____

What are the three goals you will implement to stop blaming others?

_____
_____
_____

What action steps will you take to move you forward?

___

___

___

5.7 Reflection:

What triggers plunge you into fear and unforgiveness (For example: practicing negative habits and making negative comments).

___

___

___

Appendix 2
Daily Accomplishment Sheet

Monthly calendar

Write five goals on the calendar that you want to achieve this month and at the end of the month check off the goals you achieved and move the ones you did not achieve to the next month.

MONDAY	TUESDAY	WEDNESDAY	THURSDAY	FRIDAY	SATURDAY	SUNDAY
1	2	3	4	5	6	7
8	9	10	11	12	13	14
15	16	17	18	19	20	21
22	23	24	25	26	27	28
29	30	31				

SECTION #6
Self-Awareness

"The first step toward change is awareness. The second step is acceptance."
—Nathaniel Brandon

6.1 Definition

Self-awareness refers to the ability to recognize and understand one's thoughts, feelings, sensations, and actions. It involves introspection and a conscious perception of oneself as an individual separate from others.

Here are some critical points about self-awareness: It involves being conscious of your-existence, including your emotions, desires, beliefs, and behaviors. Self-awareness is linked to personal growth and development. By understanding oneself better, you can:

Set meaningful goals.	Make intentional choices aligned with your values.	Work towards becoming the best version of yourself.

6.2 Benefits

Self-awareness and forgiveness are the initial processes that opens doors of communication and intimacy. Notice what you are noticing. In other words, pay attention to where your mind wanders.

6.3 Naikan Therapy

Naikan therapy focuses on self-reflection. This therapy requires you to concentrate on three questions:

(1) What have you received from your partner?

_____

_____

(2) What have you given back to your partner?

_____
_____
_____

(3) What trouble have you caused your partner?

_____
_____
_____

6.3 The role of mindfulness

Self-awareness refers to the ability to recognize and understand one's-thoughts, feelings, sensations, and actions. It involves introspection, a conscious perception of oneself separate from others. Self-awareness consists of being conscious of your existence, including your emotions, desires, beliefs, and behaviors. It is the foundation for introspection and self-reflection.

Three Goals to help you become more self-aware (Example: paying attention to my thoughts)

_____
_____
_____

Action Steps that assist you in becoming self-aware (Example: practice self-awareness)

_____
_____
_____

Do you accept responsibility for your actions?

_____

_____

_____

6.4 Reflection Question

Using the Naikan theory,-consider an incident that happened in your relationship and answer the three questions.

(1) What you have received.

_____

_____

_____

(2) What you have returned.

_____

_____

_____

(3) What trouble you caused.

_____

_____

_____

Appendix 2
Daily Accomplishment Sheet

Monthly Calendar

Write five goals on the calendar that you want to reach this month and at the end of the month, check off the goals you achieved and move the ones you did not to the next month.

MONDAY	TUESDAY	WEDNESDAY	THURSDAY	FRIDAY	SATURDAY	SUNDAY
1	2	3	4	5	6	7
8	9	10	11	12	13	14
15	16	17	18	19	20	21
22	23	24	25	26	27	28
29	30	31				

SECTION #7
Mind Reset

"Whether you think you can or you think you can't, you're right."
—Henry Ford

7.1 Definition

Mind reset refers to intentionally clearing and refreshing one's mind, often to relieve stress, gain clarity, or improve focus. It involves consciously shifting your focus, thoughts, and attention to create a mental break from your current state. It is a way to reset and recharge your mind, like restarting a computer to optimize its performance.

7.2 Benefits of Mind Reset

Mind reset assists in clearing mental clutter and releasing excessive thoughts, worries, and distractions. Mind reset allows you to let go of mental baggage, creating space for new ideas and perspectives.

7.3 Techniques for resetting the mind.

Remember that mind reset practices can vary from person to person, and it's important to find techniques that resonate with you and support your well-being. Adapt and adjust these techniques based on your individual preferences and circumstances.

There are several ways to reset your mind:

Practicing meditation exercises helps calm the mind, increase self-awareness, and promote mental clarity.

Slow deep breathing exercises can activate the body's relaxation response, reducing stress and promoting a sense of calmness.

Physical exercise, walking, and running can help clear the mind by increasing oxygen flow to the brain and releasing endorphins.

Taking a break from electronic devices and digital distractions allows you to disconnect from external stimuli and create space for introspection and reflection.

Pursuing activities you enjoy, such as painting, playing a musical instrument, or writing, can provide a mental reset by diverting your attention and fostering a flow state.

Spending time in nature: Being in nature has a calming effect on the mind and can promote relaxation, reduce stress, and enhance mental well-being.

Resetting the mind helps alleviate stress and anxiety by providing a mental break and promoting relaxation.

Clearing the mind allows for enhanced focus, concentration, and mental clarity, leading to increased task productivity and efficiency.

A reset can stimulate creativity by opening space for new ideas and perspectives.

Resetting the mind can help regulate emotions, improve mood, and foster greater well-being.

Mind resets are most effective when practiced regularly. Setting aside dedicated time for self-care, relaxation, and reflection can prevent mental burnout and promote overall mental well-being.

You can combine different techniques for mind reset to create a personalized routine that suits your preferences and needs. Experimenting with various methods can help identify the most effective strategies for you.

7.4 Overcoming Mental Blocks

Overcoming mental blocks in relationships is a personal journey, and progress may take time. Be patient and compassionate with yourself as you work towards healthier and more fulfilling connections.

Here are some strategies that may help you navigate and overcome these blocks.

- **Self-reflection**
  Reflect on past experiences or traumas that may influence your present situation.

- **Identify specific mental blocks**
  or fears in intimacy, trust, or vulnerability.

- Have open and **honest communication.**

- **Challenge negative thoughts**
  by questioning their validity, then replace negative self-talk with positive and affirming statements.

Set realistic expectations and be willing to compromise.

Start by taking small steps outside of your comfort zone. Be patient because change can take time.

What are your three goals of mind reset?

_____
_____
_____

Action Step: How will you implement the goals you set?

_____
_____
_____

7.5 Reflection Question:
How will you intentionally reset or clear your mind?

_____
_____
_____

Appendix 2
Daily Accomplishment Sheet

Monthly Calendar

Write five goals on the calendar that you want to reach this month, and at the end of the month, check off the goals you achieved and move the ones you did not achieve to the next month.

MONDAY	TUESDAY	WEDNESDAY	THURSDAY	FRIDAY	SATURDAY	SUNDAY
1	2	3	4	5	6	7
8	9	10	11	12	13	14
15	16	17	18	19	20	21
22	23	24	25	26	27	28
29	30	31				

SECTION #8
Conflict Resolution

*"Because people aren't perfect and relationships are messy,
we all need to learn how to resolve conflicts."*
— John Maxwell

8.1 Definition

Conflict resolution refers to the process of addressing and resolving disputes and disagreements. It involves finding mutually satisfactory solutions and fostering positive relationships.

Here are some critical points on conflict resolution:

- Address conflicts calmly and constructively, focusing on finding solutions rather than winning arguments.

- Compromising and finding common ground is essential for resolving differences.

8.2 Sources of Conflict

The origin of conflicts arises from differences in values, goals, interests, communication styles, or competing needs. Resolving conflicts is crucial for maintaining healthy relationships, promoting teamwork and collaboration, and preventing the escalation of disputes. It fosters understanding and cooperation.

8.3 Strategies for finding common ground.

Listed below are some strategies for conflict resolution:

- **Communication:** Open and honest communication is essential for resolving conflicts. Active listening, expressing thoughts and feelings clearly, and seeking to understand the perspectives of others are critical components of effective communication.

- **Collaboration:** Encouraging collaborative problem-solving allows all parties to actively participate in finding a solution. It involves identifying shared goals, exploring options, and working together toward a mutually beneficial outcome.

- **Compromise:** Sometimes, finding a middle ground through understanding is necessary. Each party may need to make concessions and find a solution that partially meets their needs and interests.

- **Emotional intelligence:** Developing emotional intelligence, including self-awareness and empathy, aids in understanding and managing emotions during conflicts. It allows you to navigate difficult emotions, maintain self-control, and show compassion towards others involved in a difference of opinion.

- **Brainstorming:** Applying problem-solving techniques, such as brainstorming or using decision-making frameworks like SWOT analysis (Strengths, Weaknesses, Opportunities, Threats), can help generate creative solutions and objectively evaluate different options.

8.4 Steps in conflict resolution:

- **Identify the conflict:** Identify and define the conflict, including the parties involved, the issues at stake, and the desired outcomes.

- **Understand perspectives:** Encourage all parties to express their viewpoints and concerns. Foster active listening and empathy to each party's needs, interests, and underlying motivations.

- **Explore solutions:** Brainstorm and explore different solutions that address the underlying issues. Encourage open dialogue and creative thinking to generate a variety of options.

- **Evaluate and choose:** Assess the pros and cons of each potential solution. Choose the solution that best meets the needs of all parties and has the highest chances of success.

- **Implement and follow up:** Develop an action plan for implementing the chosen solution. Establish a follow-up process to evaluate the effectiveness of the resolution and adjust if necessary.

Build a positive conflict resolution culture: Creating an environment that supports healthy conflict resolution is essential. Encourage open communication, establish clear expectations for respectful behavior, provide training on conflict resolution skills, and promote a culture that values cooperation and problem-solving.

Resolving conflicts plays a crucial role in relationships allowing couples to express their concerns, listen to each other's viewpoints, and find mutually acceptable resolutions.

Three goals of resolving conflict (Example: I will think before I open my mouth)

_____

_____

_____

Action Steps: How will you implement your stated goals?

_____

_____

_____

What is the number one reason you have conflicts with your spouse?

_____

_____

_____

8.5 Reflection Question
What steps do you take to resolve conflicts in your relationship?

_____

_____

_____

See Appendix 2
Daily Accomplishment Sheet

Monthly Calendar

Write five goals on the calendar that you want to achieve this month, and at the end of the month, check off the goals you achieved and move the ones you did not perform-to the next month.

MONDAY	TUESDAY	WEDNESDAY	THURSDAY	FRIDAY	SATURDAY	SUNDAY
1	2	3	4	5	6	7
8	9	10	11	12	13	14
15	16	17	18	19	20	21
22	23	24	25	26	27	28
29	30	31				

SECTION #9
Embracing Change

"Change can be hard. It requires no extra effort to settle for the same old thing. Auto-pilot keeps us locked into past patterns. But transforming your life? That requires courage, commitment, and effort. It's tempting to stay camped in the zone of That's-Just-How-It-Is. But to get to the good stuff in life, you have to be willing to become an explorer and adventurer. Transforming your life into something better requires a conscious investment of purposeful action."
—John Mark Green

9.1 Nature of Change

Embracing change in relationships refers to the willingness and ability to adapt, grow, and navigate through transitions and transformations within interpersonal connections. Recognize that change is unavoidable and a natural part of life and relationships. Accepting change is inevitable helps you approach it with an open and adaptive mindset.

9.2 Benefits of Change

Change brings opportunities for personal growth and development. Embrace the chance to learn and evolve as individuals within the relationship, recognizing that personal growth can positively impact the dynamics and quality of the connection.

Understand that maintaining open and honest communication is crucial when navigating relationship changes. Express your thoughts, feelings, and concerns, and actively listen to your partner's perspectives because clear and respectful communication promotes understanding and enables the relationship to adapt to new circumstances.

Embracing change requires flexibility and adaptability. Release old patterns or routines that may no longer serve the relationship and be open to trying new approaches. Flexibility allows for exploration and adjustment as the relationship evolves.

As relationships change, it is essential to manage expectations. Recognize that you and your spouse may evolve differently and that the relationship dynamics may shift accordingly. Adjusting expectations and being flexible can help alleviate potential conflicts and disappointments.

9.3 Struggles of Change

Change can sometimes bring uncertainty and challenges. Nurture trust and understanding in the relationship by maintaining a solid-foundation of open communication, empathy, and support. Trust and compassion-provide a sense of security and resilience during change. As individuals change and grow, the relationship should blossom to align with both partners' aspirations and values. Regularly discuss and reaffirm your shared vision for the future.

9.4 Growth Mindset

Don't be timid; embracing change involves exploring new experiences as a couple, engaging in activities or hobbies outside your comfort zone, fostering shared growth, and creating new bonds within the relationship.

List three ways you have changed during your relationship.

_____
_____
_____

What is your number one goal of change?

_____
_____
_____

How will you implement the goal?

_____
_____
_____

9.5 Reflection Question:
Why do you think you struggle with change?

_____

_____

_____

See Appendix 2
Daily Accomplishment Sheet

Monthly Calendar
Write five goals on the calendar that you want to achieve this month, and at the end of the month, check off the goals you achieved and move the ones you did not perform-to the next month.

MONDAY	TUESDAY	WEDNESDAY	THURSDAY	FRIDAY	SATURDAY	SUNDAY
1	2	3	4	5	6	7
8	9	10	11	12	13	14
15	16	17	18	19	20	21
22	23	24	25	26	27	28
29	30	31				

SECTION #10
Inner Healing

"Healing yourself is connected to healing others."
—Yoko

Overview: This chapter will introduce inner healing and its connection to achieving effective communication.

10.1 Definition

Inner healing in relationships refers to addressing and healing emotional wounds, past traumas, and personal issues that may impact the quality and dynamics of relationships. Here are some notes on inner healing in relationships.

10.2 Connections between past and present

Inner healing involves acknowledging and addressing past wounds, traumas, or emotional baggage that-impact your current relationships. This may require seeking therapy, counseling, or other supportive resources to process and heal from these experiences. The pathway to inner healing involves cultivating self-awareness as you reflect on your thoughts, emotions, and behaviors. Becoming self-aware allows you to understand the root causes of emotional wounds and begin the healing process. Have compassion for yourself and be gentle and patient as you navigate the healing journey. Treat yourself with kindness, understanding, and love, recognizing that healing takes time and effort.

Next, develop healthy strategies for emotional regulation, which involves learning to identify and manage emotions while responding to triggers and conflicts.

Establishing and maintaining healthy boundaries is crucial for inner healing and healthy relationships. Clearly define and communicate your needs, limits, and expectations within relationships. Respect and honor your boundaries and encourage others to do the same.

Inner healing often involves letting go of resentment and practicing forgiveness. Holding onto grudges or unresolved anger can hinder personal growth and strain relationships. Forgiveness allows for emotional release and promotes healing and reconciliation.

Inner healing in relationships involves developing a deep sense of self-love and self-worth. Nurture your physical, emotional, and mental well-being, and engage in self-care practices that promote self-love and self-acceptance.

You can contribute to healthier, more fulfilling relationships when you love and value yourself.

Don't hesitate to seek support from trusted friends, family members, or professionals during your inner healing journey. Engaging in therapy, counseling, or support groups can provide guidance, insights, and tools to facilitate healing and personal growth within relationships.

Inner healing is an ongoing process that requires continuous growth and reflection. Regularly assess your emotional well-being, identify areas that may still need healing or improvement, and engage in practices that promote self-growth and inner healing.

Goals of inner healing with examples:

_____

_____

_____

Action Steps How will you implement your goals?

_____

_____

_____

Do you believe your spouse can change? Why or why not?

_____

_____

_____

10.3 Reflection Question:
List three things you need to be healed from emotionally.

_____
_____
_____

See Appendix 2
Daily Accomplishment Sheet

Monthly Calendar
Write five goals on the calendar that you want to achieve this month, and at the end of the month, check off the goals you achieved and move the ones you did not perform-to the next month.

MONDAY	TUESDAY	WEDNESDAY	THURSDAY	FRIDAY	SATURDAY	SUNDAY
1	2	3	4	5	6	7
8	9	10	11	12	13	14
15	16	17	18	19	20	21
22	23	24	25	26	27	28
29	30	31				

APPENDIX 1
Self-Care Assessment Plan

Self-care is essential for maintaining your physical, emotional, and mental well-being. This assessment plan will help you evaluate your current self-care practices and develop a personalized improvement plan. Follow the steps below to create your self-care assessment plan:

Reflect on your current self-care practices. Take some time to reflect on how you currently prioritize self-care in your life. Consider the following areas:

- **Physical Self-Care:** How well do you care for your body through exercise, nutrition, sleep, and hygiene?

- **Emotional Self-Care:** How do you manage and express your emotions? Do you engage in activities that bring you joy and fulfillment?

- **Mental Self-Care:** Are you engaging in activities stimulating your mind and supporting your intellectual growth? Do you practice mindfulness or engage in activities that help reduce stress?

- **Social Self-Care:** How do you nurture relationships and maintain a support system? Do you engage in meaningful connections with others?

- **Spiritual Self-Care:** Do you engage in activities that align with your values and beliefs? How do you find meaning and purpose in your life?

APPENDIX 2
Daily Accomplishment Sheet

Something I did well today…	
Today I had fun when…	
I felt proud when…	
Today I accomplished…	
I had a positive experience with…	
Something I did for someone…	
I felt good about myself when…	
I was proud of someone else…	
Today was interesting because…	
I felt proud when…	
A positive thing I witnessed…	
Today I accomplished…	
Something I did well today…	
I had a positive experience with (a person, place, or thing) …	
I was proud of someone when…	
Today I had fun when…	
Something I did for someone…	
I felt good about myself when…	

A positive thing I witnessed…	
Today was interesting because…	
I felt proud when…	

APPENDIX 3

BARRIERS TO COMMUNICATION		
1. Interrupting 2. Dominating the conversation 3. Using aggressive language	4. Failing to listen actively. 5. Being defensive 6. Poor listening skills	7. Overly emotional 8. Focusing on the person instead of the behavior 9. Expecting mind-reading

APPENDIX 4

Here are some suggestions of things to embrace when you find it hard to forgive:

- Show some sympathy.

- Journal about it.

- What has been done cannot be undone, so control your anger and fear.

- Focus on what might work and try to magnify that thought!

- Replace negative emotions with positive emotions!

- Think of a time when you offended someone, and you were forgiven.

- Visualize your husband sitting across from you and tell him what you want him to know.

- Recognize the part, conscious or unconscious, you have contributed to the situation.

APPENDIX 5

SIGNS OF POOR COMMUNICATION		
1. Interrupting 2. Dominating the conversation 3. Using aggressive language	4. Failing to listen actively. 5. Being defensive 6. Poor listening skills	7. Overly emotional 8. Focusing on the person instead of the behavior 9. Expecting mind-reading

APPENDIX 6

AFFIRMATION BY GANDHI
💛 I will keep my thoughts positive.
💛 Because my thoughts become my words
💛 I will keep my words positive.
💛 Because my words become my habits
💛 I will keep my habits positive.
💛 Because my habits become my values
💛 I will keep my habits positive.
💛 Because my values become my destiny

APPENDIX 7

Fill in the blank Affirmation 1

I am thankful for _____

I deserve _____

I attract _____

I will try _____

I trust _____

I choose to focus on _____

I am ready to embrace _____

I am open to _____

NOTES

NOTES

NOTES

NOTES

NOTES